| DATE | | | |
|------|------|------|------|
| FEB 1994 | | | |
| | | | |
| | | | |
| | | | |
| | | | |
| | | | |
| | | | |
| | | | |
| | | | |
| | | | |

 FEB 1991

BAKER & TAYLOR BOOKS

# CARS AND HOW THEY GO

by JOANNA COLE       illustrated by GAIL GIBBONS

HarperCollins*Publishers*

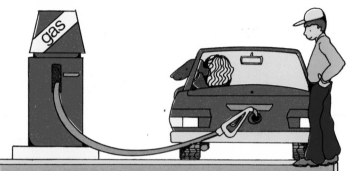

For his careful checking of the text and illustrations,
the author and artist thank James R. Rose of the Ford Motor Company.

Text copyright © 1983 by Joanna Cole
Illustrations copyright © 1983 by Gail Gibbons
All rights reserved.
Printed in the United States of America.

Library of Congress Cataloging in Publication Data
Cole, Joanna.
  Cars and how they go.

  Summary: Briefly describes the operations of all
the working parts of an automobile.
  1. Automobiles—Juvenile literature.
[1. Automobiles.   2. Engines]  I. Gibbons, Gail,
ill.  II. Title
TL147.C54  1983        629.2'222        82-45575
ISBN 0-690-04261-2
ISBN 0-690-04262-0 (lib. bdg.)

6  7  8  9  10

It's a shiny new car with a full tank of gas. When the driver turns the key, presses down on the gas pedal, and moves the gearshift lever, the car will start to move.

The car moves because the wheels turn. In the days before cars, wagons and carriages were pulled by horses. The horse's power turned the wheels.

The people who invented cars had a problem to solve: how to make a carriage that could turn its own wheels. They solved the problem by building an engine that made its own power.

Under the car's hood, the engine makes the power that will make the wheels go around.

The engine turns a rod called a crankshaft. The crankshaft is connected to another rod, the drive shaft, that reaches from the front of the car to the rear. The drive shaft is connected to the rear axle, a rod that holds the rear wheels on.

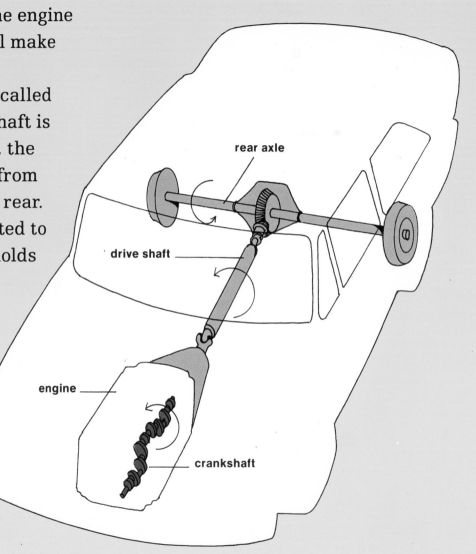

rear axle

drive shaft

engine

crankshaft

The crankshaft turns the drive shaft.
The drive shaft turns the rear axle.
And the rear axle turns the rear wheels.
    As they go around, the front wheels
turn too, and the car moves.

But how does the engine make the power to turn the crankshaft in the first place? It makes power by burning gasoline.

A car also has headlights for night driving...
turn signals, stoplights, backup lights, and a horn for warning
other drivers...

wipers and blowers to keep the windshield clear...
seat belts to protect passengers in case of accidents...

In cars with disk brakes, a metal disk is attached to each wheel. Over the disk is a large clamp. When the driver steps on the brake pedal, the sides of the clamp are pushed together. They pinch the disk like a thumb and forefinger and stop the wheel.

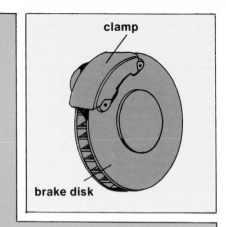

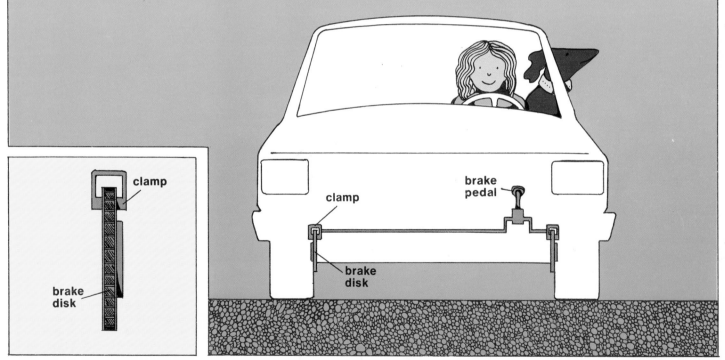

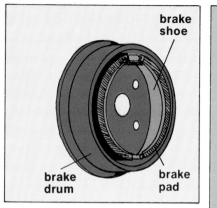

brake shoe
brake drum
brake pad

In cars with drum brakes, each wheel has a metal lining called a brake drum. When the driver steps on the brake pedal, the pressure travels through brake lines to padded metal brake "shoes." The shoes are pushed outward against the drum, stopping the wheel.

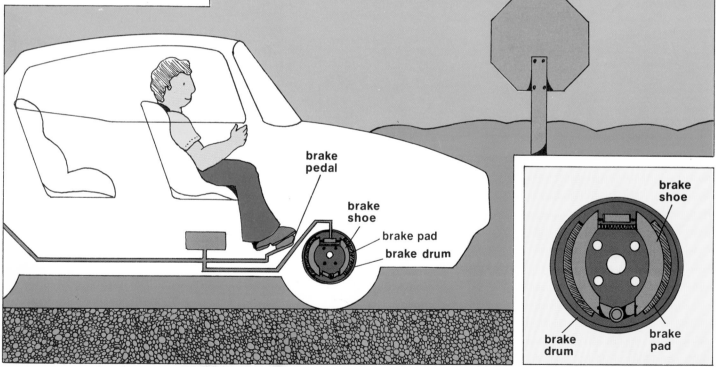

brake pedal
brake shoe
brake pad
brake drum

brake shoe
brake drum
brake pad

To stop the car, the driver steps on the brake pedal.

There are two kinds of brakes, drum brakes and disk brakes.

Most cars have drum brakes.

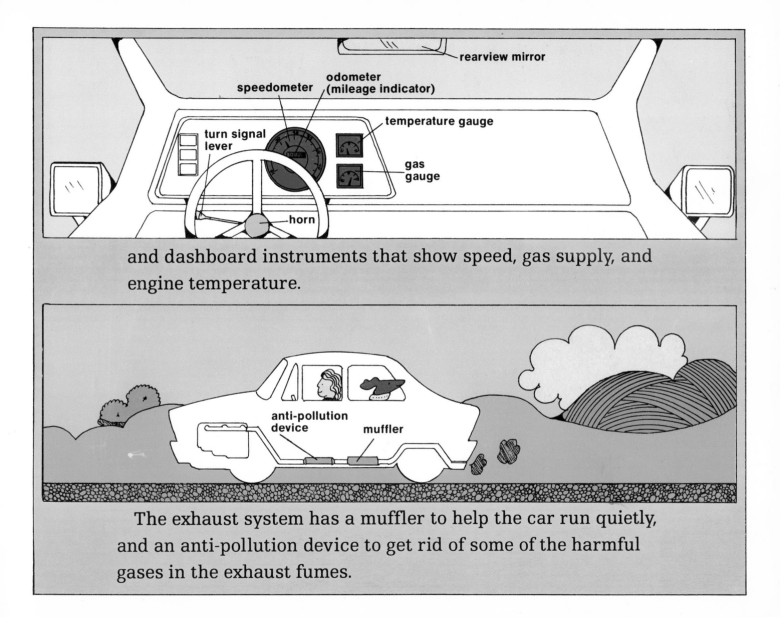

and dashboard instruments that show speed, gas supply, and engine temperature.

The exhaust system has a muffler to help the car run quietly, and an anti-pollution device to get rid of some of the harmful gases in the exhaust fumes.

Not every car is exactly like the one we have shown here. In some cars, the gears shift automatically. In some, the engine turns the front wheels instead of the rear ones. And in others, the engine is cooled by air instead of water.

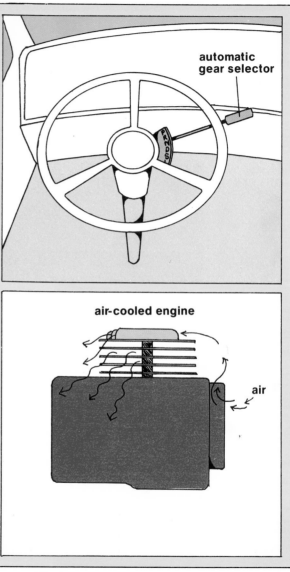

automatic gear selector

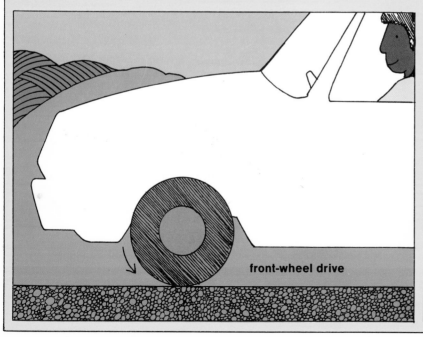

front-wheel drive

air-cooled engine

air

Some cars have different kinds of engines altogether. The rotary engine has a rotor— turning part—that is pushed around by the force of the exploding gas vapor.

The diesel engine burns oil instead of gasoline. Most trucks have diesel engines.

The gas turbine engine works like a rocket: a jet of hot gas spins a many-bladed fan (turbine) to turn the wheels.

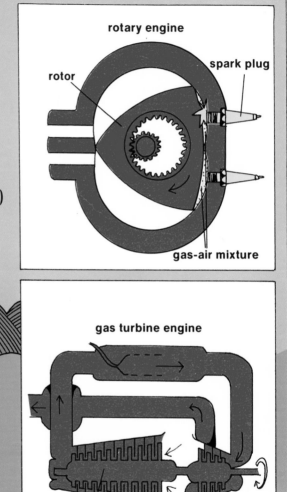

rotary engine

rotor

spark plug

gas-air mixture

gas turbine engine

turbine

diesel engine

Cars keep changing as people find new ways of building them. One day we may drive cars that run on electric batteries or that burn alcohol instead of gasoline. Or some day cars might be solar-powered, using the energy of the sun.

But no matter what cars are like in the future, they will always need a power source to make the wheels go around. Because that's how cars go.

The gas is burned in cylinders. There are four, six, or eight cylinders in an engine—usually, a car with more cylinders will make more power.

Each cylinder is an upside-down container about the size of a jelly jar. Fitted inside the cylinder is a piston, which goes up and down like a plug.

The cylinders and pistons are the engine's power source.

engine

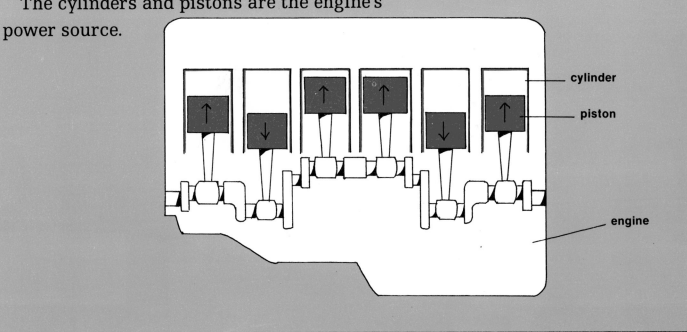

cylinder

piston

engine

When the driver steps on the gas pedal, gasoline is pumped from the fuel tank through a pipe to the carburetor. The carburetor mixes the gas with air to make a mist, or vapor, the way an atomizer makes a mist of perfume.

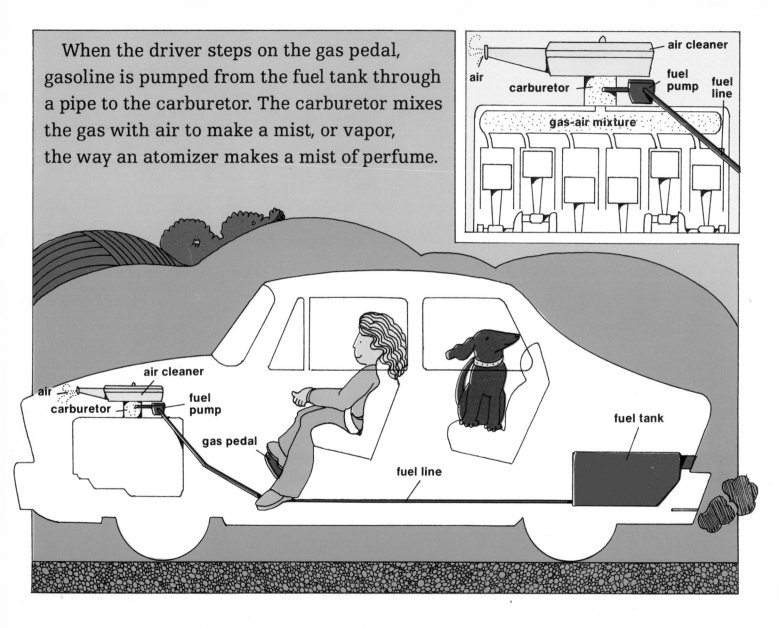

The gas vapor goes from the carburetor to the cylinders. At the top of each cylinder is a valve, which acts like a little door: it opens to let in the vapor.

When the cylinder is filled with vapor, the valve closes. The piston goes up and compresses—squeezes—the vapor into the small space at the top.

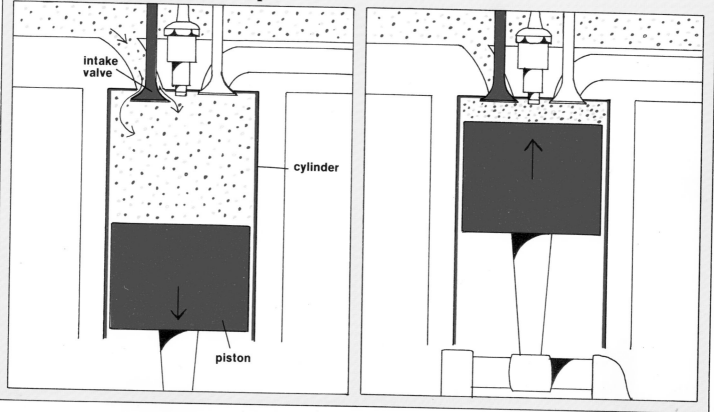

intake valve

cylinder

piston

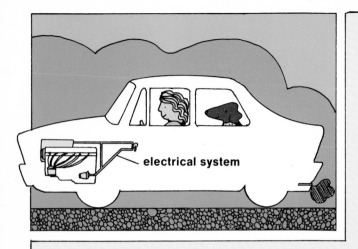

electrical system

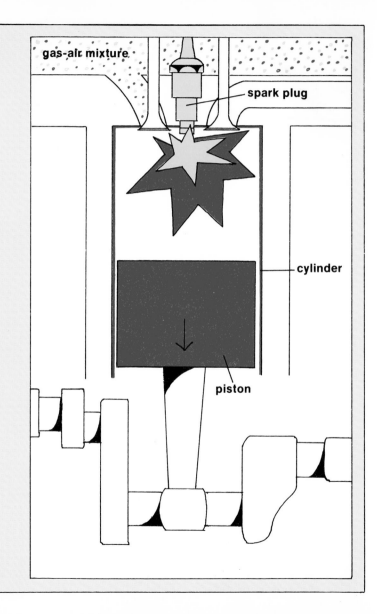

gas-air mixture

spark plug

cylinder

piston

To set the vapor burning, each cylinder has a spark plug, which gets electricity from the car's electrical system. When the piston goes up, the spark plug gives off an electrical spark, which ignites the vapor.

Because the vapor is compressed, it doesn't burn slowly. It explodes—bang! The explosion shoves the piston down hard.

exhaust

exhaust
valve

After the explosion, the cylinder is full of burned-up gas vapor. A second valve opens to let out the burned vapor, called exhaust.

The exhaust from all the cylinders goes through a system of pipes and out the tail pipe of the car.

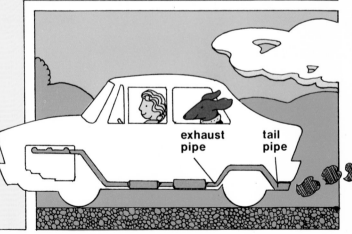

exhaust
pipe

tail
pipe

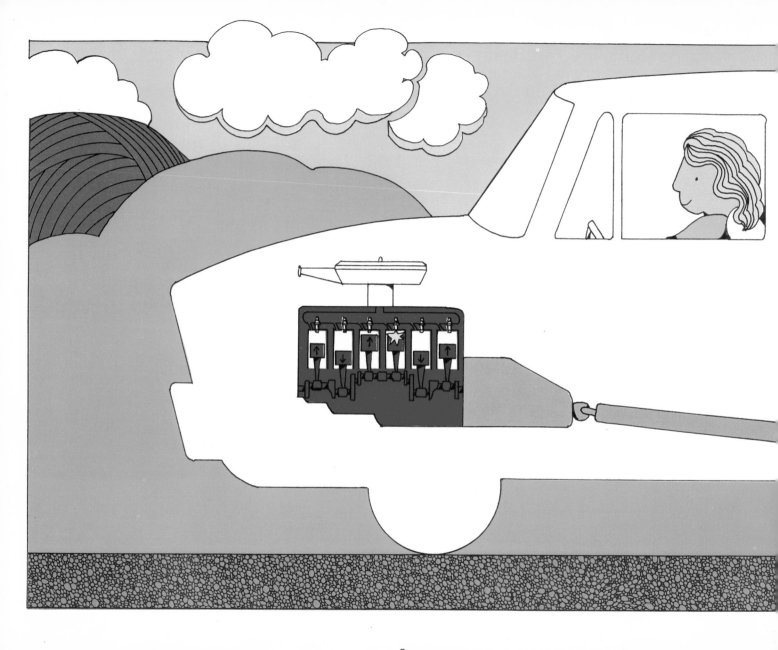

When the car is running, there are hundreds of explosions every minute. The explosions push the pistons down with a great deal of force. This "push" is the power that goes from the engine to turn the rear wheels.

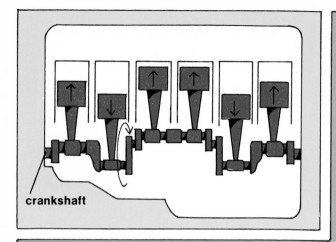

crankshaft

It takes several steps for the engine's power to reach the rear wheels. First, the pistons turn the crankshaft.

The crankshaft is made in sections, and each section is connected to a piston. When the piston moves up and down, it turns its section of the crankshaft round and round.

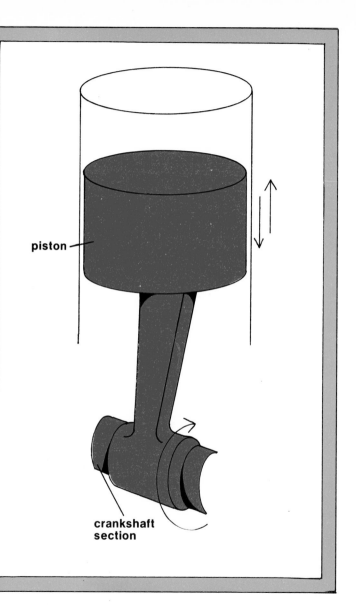

piston

crankshaft section

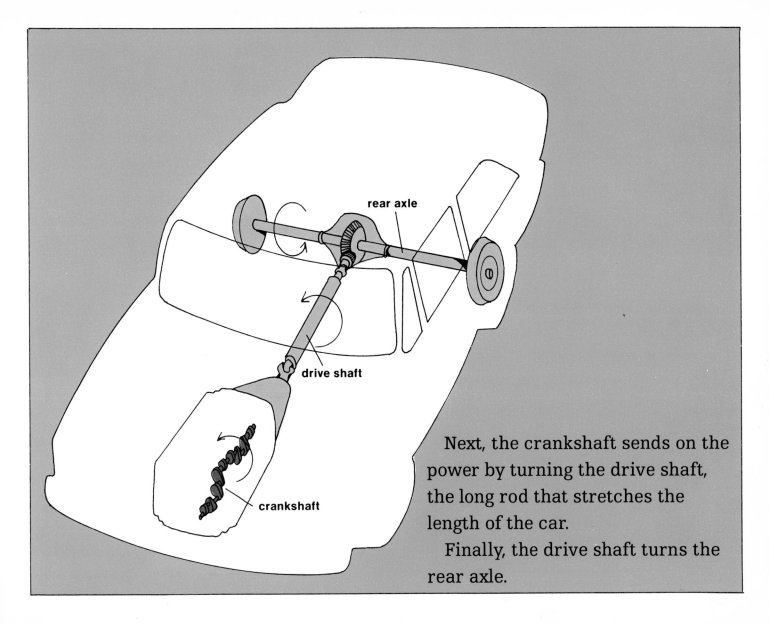

rear axle

drive shaft

crankshaft

Next, the crankshaft sends on the power by turning the drive shaft, the long rod that stretches the length of the car.

Finally, the drive shaft turns the rear axle.

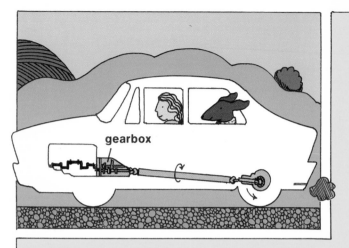

gearbox

The crankshaft, the drive shaft, and the rear axle are all connected to each other by gears—metal wheels with teeth, or notches, on their edges. The teeth of one gear mesh with—fit into—the teeth of another. When one gear turns, it makes the other gear turn, too.

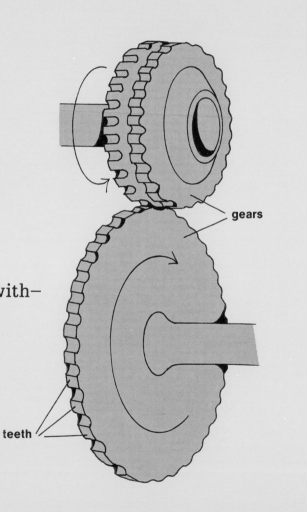

gears

teeth

There are several gears that connect the crankshaft to the drive shaft—gears for going forward at different speeds and a reverse gear for going backward. To select the gear he wants, the driver steps on the clutch pedal and moves the gearshift lever. When the car is "in gear," the crankshaft turns the gears, and the gears turn the drive shaft.

The turning power of the drive shaft is passed on to the rear axle and wheels by another set of gears.

clutch

gearshift lever

crankshaft

gears

clutch pedal

drive shaft

rear gears

rear axle

And that's how a car goes. When the engine is running, each part turns another to make the wheels go around.

But the engine cannot get started by itself.

In old-time cars, the driver had to turn the crankshaft with a handle to get the engine going.

In today's cars, a small electric motor—the starter—turns the crankshaft.

When the driver turns the key, the car's battery runs the starter. Once the gas begins firing in the engine's cylinders, the starter shuts off. The engine is running on its own power.

battery

ignition key

crankshaft

starter motor

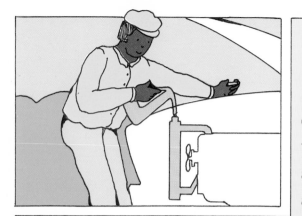

As the engine runs, it gets very hot. To get rid of heat, there is a cooling system. Water is pumped through pipes around the cylinders. The water draws off heat. Then the water flows back to a radiator, a container at the front of the engine, where it is cooled again by a fan.

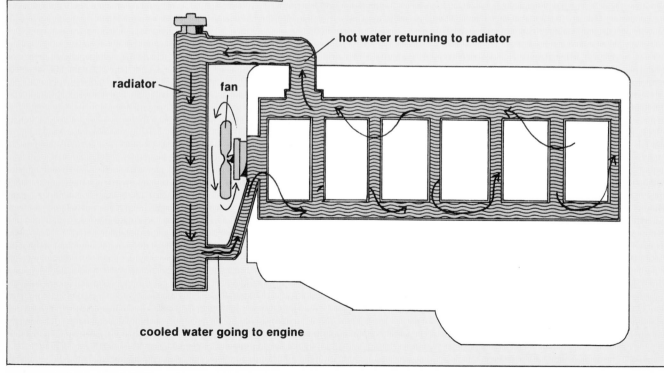

hot water returning to radiator

radiator

fan

cooled water going to engine

The engine also has a lubrication system to keep it running smoothly. Oil is pumped from an oil pan and sprayed on the moving parts. The oil keeps the parts from wearing each other down and from getting too hot as they rub together.

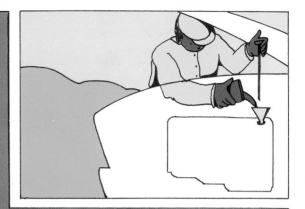

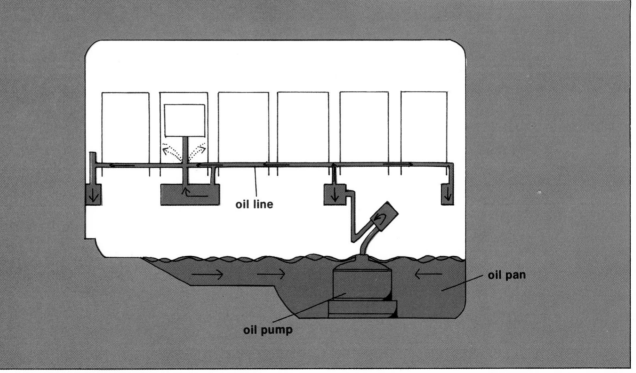

oil line

oil pan

oil pump

On the road, the driver controls the car by turning the steering wheel. The shaft of the steering wheel is connected by gears to rods that link the front wheels. The steering gears push the rods to one side or the other and make the front wheels turn left or right.

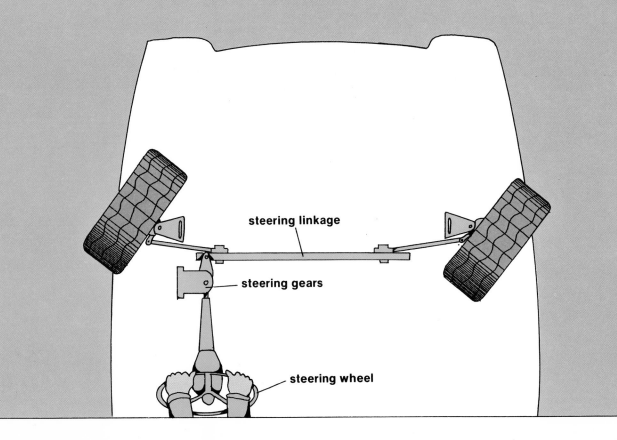

steering linkage

steering gears

steering wheel